FREEDOM FROM EXPLOITATION

Other Snapshot Series Books

People, Trees and Poverty
A Snapshot of Environmental Missions

Lowell Bliss (Author)

People, Trees & Poverty shares a high-level overview of what it looks like to reach the unreached through advocacy on environmental issues. However, this book does more than raise awareness and pluck your heartstrings. It concludes with a critical feature, listing additional resources, gatherings, and organizations to move the reader from concern to action.

It's Your Call
To a Missional or Missionary Life

David P. Jacob (Author)

For most believers, several factors influence their missions call. Some are called to stay in their hometown and support missions at their local church, others are called to short-term mission trips, while others are called to spend a lifetime overseas. *It's Your Call* highlights three things that can help you discover the adventure God has for you in his mission: prayer and Bible study, missionary mentorship, and short-term mission trips.

Insiders and Alongsiders
An Invitation to the Conversation

Kevin Higgins (Author)

In *Insiders and Alongsiders*, Kevin Higgins offers his evolving perspective on "insider" movements (IMs), a controversial type of movement in which families and friendship networks become faithful followers of Jesus while remaining identified with the culture of their people group.

Effective Spiritual Warfare
Wrestling in God's Strength

Mary Lou Codman-WIlson (Author)

Effective Spiritual Warfare describes the tactics evil forces use to keep Christians from fulfilling God's plans for them personally and globally. Then the book concentrates primarily on eight ways to overcome Satan in our lives. These principles are truly life transforming, thoroughly biblical, and consistently validated throughout Christian history.

FREEDOM FROM EXPLOITATION

Christian Responses to Modern-Day Slavery

Marion L. S. Carson

Freedom from Exploitation: Christian Responses to Modern-Day Slavery

© 2023 by Marion L. S. Carson. All Rights Reserved.

No part of this book may be reproduced, stored in a retrieval system, or transmitted in any form or by any means—electronic, mechanical, photocopy, recording, or otherwise—without prior written permission from the publisher, except brief quotations used in connection with reviews in magazines or newspapers. For permission, email permissions@wclbooks.com. For corrections, email editor@wclbooks.com.

The material in this Snapshot book was expanded from chapter 12 of the forthcoming book *Tides of Opportunity: Missiological Experiences and Engagements in Global Migration* (Littleton, CO: William Carey Publishing).

William Carey Publishing (WCP) publishes resources to shape and advance the missiological conversation in the world. We publish a broad range of thought-provoking books and do not necessarily endorse all opinions set forth here or in works referenced within this book. WCP can't verify the accuracy of website URLs beyond the date of print publication.

All Scripture quotations, unless otherwise indicated, are taken from the Holy Bible, New International Version®, NIV®. Copyright ©1973, 1978, 1984, 2011 by Biblica, Inc.™ Used by permission of Zondervan. All rights reserved worldwide. www.zondervan.com. The "NIV" and "New International Version" are trademarks registered in the United States Patent and Trademark Office by Biblica, Inc.™

Scripture quotations marked NRSV are taken from the New Revised Standard Version Bible, copyright © 1989 National Council of the Churches of Christ in the United States of America. Used by permission. All rights reserved worldwide.

Scripture quotations taken from the NASB® New American Bible®, Copyright © 1960, 1971, 1977, 1995, 2020 by The Lockman Foundation. Used by permission. All rights reserved. lockman.org.

Published by William Carey Publishing
10 W. Dry Creek Cir
Littleton, CO 80120 | www.missionbooks.org

William Carey Publishing is a ministry of Frontier Ventures
Pasadena, CA | www.frontierventures.org

Cover and Interior Designer: Mike Riester

The Snapshot Series: Number 5

ISBNs: 978-1-64508-545-4 (paperback)
       978-1-64508-547-8 (epub)

Printed Worldwide
27 26 25 24 23   1 2 3 4 5   IN

Contents

Introduction	vii
1. The Story of a Victim	1
2. Learning from History	7
3. Our Role	11
4. What about Us?	19
5. A Challenge to Ourselves	27
Bibliography	31
Get Involved	33

Introduction

There are millions of victims of trafficking all over the world. They are the victims of people who exploit the vulnerable, whether it be because of poverty, war, natural disaster, or family break up (among other things). Throughout the world, too, many Christians are involved in helping these victims—in lobbying, in rescue initiatives, in rehabilitative and therapeutic work. Such work is vital.

But how can Christians help prevent such suffering in the first place? How can we contribute to the prevention of the unspeakable suffering which human trafficking causes in the lives of so many? In America, in the years before the Civil War, Quakers were inspired by the "Golden Rule" to stand up against the religious and cultural norms of their day and play a crucial part in the abolition movement. What started as an isolated voice eventually became a chorus of those who wanted to bring an end to the injustice of slavery which was so much an accepted part of society.

Today, we too can speak out against slavery, in all its forms. But are we willing to challenge the prevailing norms, both in society as a whole and within our own faith communities? Are we willing to make sacrificial changes in our own lives in order to help bring about an end to injustice in the lives of others? In this book, we will first consider the story of one victim of human trafficking and then, drawing on the example of the antebellum Quakers, ask ourselves how our Christian communities can play a part in the prevention of the unspeakable suffering and outrage which is modern-day slavery.

The Story of a Victim

He had arrived in Glasgow via London on the overnight bus. Over a hot cup of coffee in our city center drop-in—Glasgow City Mission in Scotland—with the aid of a volunteer who could speak his language, he told us some of his story.[1] He had left Africa for Europe in order to escape terrorism and warfare and had somehow managed to find his way to Belgium. He had hoped that he would be able to claim asylum, acculturate, and make a life for himself in Europe. But like so many others, he found himself vulnerable to exploitation.

He was delighted when a Belgian farmer offered him employment and worked hard for him for many weeks. Along with some others, he was given very basic accommodation and was provided with food. For a while it seemed to be a good arrangement, but it soon became obvious that the farmer had no

---

1 The author serves as Chaplain at Glasgow City Mission in Glasgow, Scotland. The oldest City Mission in the world, it was founded in 1826 by David Nasmith who went on to set up similar missions throughout the United Kingdom and in America. Today, in Glasgow, staff and volunteers reach out to people affected by poverty, homelessness, and addictions, as well as asylum seekers and refugees.

intention of paying him. When he asked for his wages, he was told that accommodation and food was all the payment he would be getting. He decided he should leave—but where could he go? He opted for the United Kingdom. After a long harrowing journey by lorry, he eventually arrived in Glasgow, knowing no one and speaking no English. After several nights sleeping rough, he was exhausted, hungry, and bewildered.

According to the United Nations Protocol to Prevent, Suppress and Punish Trafficking in Persons, which is known as the Palermo Protocol,

> "Trafficking in persons" shall mean the recruitment, transportation, transfer, harboring or receipt of persons, by means of the threat or use of force or other forms of coercion, of abduction, of fraud, of deception, of the abuse of power or of a position of vulnerability or of the giving or receiving of payments or benefits to achieve the consent of a person having control of another person, for the purpose of exploitation. Exploitation shall include, at a minimum, the exploitation of the prostitution of others or other forms of sexual exploitation, forced labor or services, slavery or practices similar to slavery, servitude or removal of organs.[2]

Victims of trafficking are found all over the world. Recruited by means of coercion, deception, or force, they work in the hospitality sector, in agriculture and fisheries, on construction sites, in private homes as domestic servants, in beauty salons, and in brothels.[3] Traffickers exploit the most vulnerable in society—

---

[2] United Nations Human Rights, "Protocol to Prevent, Suppress and Punish Trafficking."

[3] Kara, *Modern Slavery*.

those in poverty, the displaced, and the young.[4] They do so because they know that they can make huge amounts of money. Slaves provide free labor for their owners who pay little or no wages and no tax, and those who have been trafficked are made to pay back any money that has been spent on them such as for travel costs, food, or equipment.

Many victims have been exploited while escaping religious or ethnic persecution or, like the man in the story above (I'll call him Thierry), fleeing war and terrorism. And their numbers are increasing. As I write, millions of people, mostly women and children, have had to leave Ukraine as a result of the invasion of their country by Russian forces. According to the United Nations Office on Drugs and Crime, "over 13,000 unaccompanied and separated children from Ukraine were registered in the European Union (EU) as of 6 May 2022, a subgroup of whom were orphaned due to the war, or were already orphans in institutional care."[5] In their displacement and desperation, they are highly vulnerable to exploitation by human traffickers who know whom to target. Early in the war it was reported that many children had gone missing on the Ukrainian-Polish border.[6]

> Unaccompanied children are highly vulnerable to exploitation by human traffickers who know whom to target.

---

[4] It is important to distinguish trafficking from smuggling. Human traffickers coerce and deceive people into working against their will. Smuggling, on the other hand, involves the payment of money by adults, often very large amounts, to be taken across borders in order to find safety and work. Children who pay money to smugglers are considered to be victims of trafficking.

[5] United Nations Office on Drugs and Crime, *Conflict in Ukraine*.

[6] Mitchell, "Thousands of Vulnerable Children."

At our drop-in center in central Glasgow, it is our privilege to be able to work with victims of exploitation, to learn something of their stories, and to help them as best we can. We are able to offer a safe space, hot meals, English language classes, and assistance in the lengthy and complex UK asylum process. During the winter months, we help them find emergency accommodation in order to prevent them from having to sleep rough on the freezing and dangerous city streets. Throughout the year we provide a temporary community in which to make friends and learn new skills, such as English language and computing. A weekly art class is particularly popular among refugees.

Working alongside social workers, housing officers, and other charitable organizations we can ensure that displaced persons are given safe accommodation as well as financial, medical, and psychological help. Some have gone through unspeakable trauma, whether at the hands of their exploiters or on the precarious and often extremely dangerous journey they have undertaken to try to find safety and a new life. They may have lost contact with family members and friends, have few possessions, and now find themselves isolated, vulnerable, and deeply lonely. Providing a safe space in which people feel valued can help them to begin to articulate their feelings and so begin to heal. For those who are believers, we provide a safe place in which they can be strengthened in their faith, through regular Bible studies, worship, and prayer.

> Some victims have gone through unspeakable trauma.

In Thierry's case, we were able to help him find the right support, and I am happy to report that life has turned around for him. Having first fled from a situation of terrorism and war, he then had to escape exploitation. Now he has started the long journey of learning how to live with the trauma of his past and in hope for a more stable life.[7]

I say it is our privilege to work with people like Thierry, and indeed it is. But we are very much aware that we are only scratching the surface of what is a tragic situation for millions of people throughout the world. Many, many more will remain enslaved for years, hidden from view, robbed of the hope of freedom, and in physical danger from those who exploit them. We are

> We are only scratching the surface of what is a tragic situation for millions of people.

also very aware that we are dealing with the damage done by those who exploit others—serving people whose lives have been wrecked by criminals who saw them only as commodities to be bought and sold, and to be used in order to make a profit. Those who do manage to escape are likely to suffer from physical and psychological wounds which will affect them for years to come. They will need a great deal of help to learn to live in freedom without becoming isolated or exploited all over again.

In our ministry, like so many others, we seek to serve the victims of exploitation and human trafficking. We are able to do so through the generous financial support of churches and individuals and the practical help of many dedicated volunteers (over 200!) who give up their time to listen to, pray with, and walk alongside people like Thierry. It is a great privilege for us to be able to do this. But we would much rather that our service was not needed. We would much rather that such exploitation and injustice did not happen at all. We believe that it is the responsibility of Christians

---

7 Hemmings, Jakobowitz, Abas, et al., "Responding to the Health Needs."

not only to work with victims, but to help prevent such suffering in the first place.

The question is, how? How can individual Christians and church communities do this? For many, it might feel like a problem that is "out there," having nothing to do with us. It seems well divorced from our everyday experience and far too complex for us to begin to tackle anyway. Most of us are unlikely to come across enslaved people in our daily lives, and we can feel ill-equipped to do anything. We know there are people like Thierry, and we would love to prevent further suffering, but what can we do about such a huge problem which affects millions throughout the world?

> It is the responsibility of Christians not only to work with victims, but to help prevent such suffering in the first place.

Learning from History

In order to help us answer this question, we can begin by looking to Christian history. We can learn a great deal from the Quakers, who in the years before the American civil war, did so much to speak out against the injustice of slavery.[8] Among Christians today, it is taken for granted that slavery is wrong. No one challenges the notion that human trafficking is unjust and that we have a moral duty to work against it. Yet, prior to its abolition in 1865, slavery was the norm, and very few people had ever thought to question it. Most Christians, like everybody else in society, took it for granted that society should be divided into slaves and slave-owners. Not only was this the natural order of things, but they also read in their Bibles that it was God-ordained. In Leviticus, for example, they read that slavery was commanded by God and that to own fellow human beings as property was part of the correct ordering of society:[9]

---

8 Carey and Plank, *Quakers and Abolition*; Soderlund, *Quakers and Slavery*.
9 Irons, *Origins of Proslavery Christianity*; Tise, *Proslavery: A History*.

> Your male and female slaves are to come from the nations around you; from them you may buy slaves. You may also buy some of the temporary residents living among you and members of their clans born in your country, and they will become your property. You can bequeath them to your children as inherited property and can make them slaves for life, but you must not rule over your fellow Israelites ruthlessly. (Lev 25:44–46)

This text and others provided Christian slaveholders with the rationale for the view that human beings could be bought and sold and become heritable property. The Bible was also used to teach those who were enslaved that they should obey their masters as a matter of divine command:

> Let all who are under the yoke of slavery regard their masters as worthy of all honor, so that the name of God and the teaching may not be blasphemed. (1 Tim 6:1 NRSV)

On the basis of Scriptures such as these, slaves were taught that their lot was the will of God. Accordingly, they should not question their masters or try to change their situation, for in so doing they would be disobeying God himself.

The Quakers, however, began to challenge this idea—how could slave ownership be compatible with the biblical principles of freedom and equality? This made them first question the practice of slaveholding among themselves and then to stand up against the values and norms of the prevailing culture, initially within their own communities and then in society as a whole. They were well aware of the biblical texts which could be used to support slavery, but as they considered the matter, the so-called "Golden Rule" became crucial to their thinking:

> So in everything, do to others what you would have them do to you, for this sums up the Law and the Prophets. (Matt 7:12)

For them, Jesus's words encapsulated all that was necessary to grasp that slavery must be against the will of God. They realized that they themselves would not want to be enslaved, and so they could not inflict this on others. So it was that in 1688, the Mennonite Quakers of Germantown, Pennsylvania wrote to their monthly meeting:

> There is a saying that we should do to all men like as we will be done ourselves: making no difference of what generation, descent or color they are.[10]

After a long struggle among themselves, for many Quakers were slaveholders, they finally came to the conclusion that slaveholding was wrong. Inevitably, their radical stance drew criticism and hostility, in particular from Christians who found support for slaveholding in the biblical writings.[11] Nevertheless, they stood up against the prevailing culture, and played a large, crucial part in the story of abolition.

---

10 Reprinted in Morgan, *Slavery in America*, 370.

11 Carson, *Human Trafficking, the Bible*.

Our Role

For us, too, the maxim "Do to others what you would have them do to you" can be the impetus to do something about modern-day slavery. Who among us would wish to be enslaved, bought and sold as a commodity, and deprived of the freedom to live and work in the way that we choose? But what can we do to help those who find themselves in this situation?

First, we can learn as much as we can about modern slavery in all its manifestations throughout the world. The US State department annual "Trafficking in Persons Report" is a good place to start.[12] Slavery is found in different forms throughout the world. The most common form is bonded labor, in which individuals and even families give themselves to work as slaves in order to repay a debt: most often, the work is never enough to pay off the loan. Another example is forced labor, in which victims are made to work against their will, under threat of violence and for no recompense. Victims of forced labor are to be found in many types of work, for example, as domestic servants, kitchen assistants, factory and

---

12 US State Department, "Trafficking in Persons Report."

construction workers. In sex trafficking, women and girls and some men, are forced to provide sexual services in brothels, strip clubs, or massage parlors. Throughout the world, too, children are victims of coercion and exploitation—forced to work as soldiers, for example, or sold into marriage.

Next, we can help our churches to see that slavery is not something remote but is taking place in their own country and even in their neighborhood. In Scotland, for example, many nail bars are staffed by trafficked people, and slaves are to be found on farms, in hotels, and at car washes. What looks legitimate on the outside can hide a reality of slavery underneath. Another common form of exploitation in Scotland is known as "county lines" in which youngsters are groomed by adults and sent around the country carrying and selling drugs. This is a form of child labor: the children themselves do not recognize that they are being exploited—until that is, they begin to rebel or want to move on, and they find that their "boss" is not as generous as they thought he was.

> What looks legitimate on the outside can hide a reality of slavery underneath.

Once we are familiar with the forms that human trafficking takes in our part of the world, we can learn to identify the signs of trafficking and work alongside the police to educate our churches to what to do if we suspect trafficking is going on. At Glasgow City Mission, we work very closely with a charity called Restore Glasgow which was set up by local Christians who came to realize that human trafficking was taking place in their own neighborhood. Restore Glasgow's calling is to educate churches about the reality of modern slavery, teaching people how to recognize the signs and know the procedures for helping people whom they suspect might

Our Role

be victims. Working in partnership with other local organizations, they are in increasing demand to give trainings to churches throughout the Glasgow area.

Many Christians may feel that they want to become more actively involved. For some, the most obvious way to contribute is to support and assist in services which enable people like Thierry to build up new lives for themselves. By volunteering with charities like Glasgow City Mission, we can bring God's love into the lives of those who have experienced years of exploitation and of being treated as less than human. We can help ensure that their immediate needs are met—providing food, clothing, and signposting to medical help when required, for example. Perhaps even more importantly, we can draw alongside them in a safe environment, providing a nurturing community for them as they become used to freedom and all that it entails. We can support such work with our financial resources and faithful prayer. We can welcome the victims of trafficking into our church communities and help them to rebuild their lives.

> We can support such work with our financial resources and faithful prayer.

These actions are good and important. It is crucial, however, that Christians who want to become involved in direct assistance to victims of trafficking do so in conjunction with others who have knowledge and experience of this kind of work. Attempting to challenge trafficking and mount rescue operations is the job of the police, not of individual believers or indeed, local churches. You should never take the law into your own hands. Joining forces with established charities and practitioners is good—an independent "savior mentality" is not. Good intentions can be dangerous in the long run; trying to rescue people or taking victims into your own home is foolish and can be very dangerous for all concerned, including the victims of human trafficking themselves. As Shayne Moore, Sandra Morgan, and Kimberley McOwen Yim insist in their helpful book, *Ending Human Trafficking: A Handbook of Strategies for the Church Today*,

> Every church and nonprofit should make a careful assessment of its expertise and resources to provide a sustainable, consistent and compassionate response that respects the intersection of public and private roles. When churches engage in the community to work with law enforcement agencies and other secular organisations, they are following a biblical pattern of being salt and light.[13]

Working in partnership, then, is crucial. We will not be salt and light if we take the law into our own hands and bring danger to the very people we are trying to help.

Besides practical "hands-on" work of this kind, there is also much that Christians can do to ensure that exploitation and enslavement are unacceptable in our societies.[14] Like the Quakers, we can join the prophetic tradition of seeking justice and mercy in our own faith communities and in the church as a whole. It is good for communities to discuss their approach to human trafficking and questions related to the issue. What is our own attitude to the fact that slavery still exists, long after its abolition? Are we open to having our comfortable

> We can join the prophetic tradition of seeking justice and mercy in our own faith communities.

---

13 Moore, Morgan, and Yim, *Ending Human Trafficking*, 5.
14 Bales, *Ending Slavery*.

Our Role

lives disrupted by a recognition of injustice and the biblical call to speak out against it? What are we to do with the fact that Scripture itself contains voices which speak in favor of slavery?

Like the Quakers, we can campaign against the injustice that is human trafficking, and become involved in awareness-raising. We can speak out against the commodification of human beings, and lobby people in power, not just in churches but the political world too. We can pray for those who are involved in business and in law-making.

Another way that we can help is by ensuring, as best we can, that the goods we buy have not come from sources in which human trafficking has played a part, for example, by buying Fairtrade products. We can boycott those companies whose goods are produced by people who are being exploited. Websites such as that of the United States Department of Labor can help you find out more about how to ensure that the items you purchase have been ethically produced and responsibly sourced.

> We can boycott those companies whose goods are produced by people who are being exploited.

We can support charities worldwide that work to rescue those who are enslaved, and we can encourage collaboration among the many organizations engaged in this work.[15] As far as prevention is concerned, those of us who live in countries in which men, women, and children are at risk of human trafficking can help to educate parents and young people about the risk, provide safe spaces where they can meet and support each other, and teach gospel values of respect and love.

---

15 Christian Organisations Against Trafficking Network (COATNET) can provide information about anti-human trafficking organizations.

So far so good—but it is not enough to identify and treat the signs and symptoms of any disease—it is important also to tackle the varied and complex factors which contribute to the existence of human trafficking in the first place.[16] The most obvious is *poverty*. Traffickers know to target people who live hand to mouth, without opportunity for education and work, under threat of homelessness, and unable to access health care. For those in situations such as these, selling a child into labor can be an attractive option.

Another factor to tackle is *inequality*—racial, social, religious, and gender-based. Youngsters who have little or no opportunity for education could find the offer to move away for work to be irresistible. Still others are vulnerable to predators who force children into becoming child soldiers, or groom them for prostitution and the sex industry. Young girls, considered to be inferior in so many societies, can be considered a financial burden and may be sold into marriage at a very young age. Where there is corruption, the prevention of exploitation of this sort can be all but impossible. And, as we have seen, displacement as a result of conflict and war renders millions of young people vulnerable to coercion, kidnapping, and all kinds of exploitation.

> People find themselves exploited because of greed for wealth and lust for power over others.

Tackling problems like these are political matters, of course, and there are many Christians who are involved in trying to change things at this level, for example, the International Justice Mission. But fundamentally, from a theological perspective, it is important to realize that human trafficking is rooted in human failings. People find themselves exploited because of greed for wealth and lust for

---

16 Enrile, *Ending Human Trafficking*, 51–70.

power over others. The corrupt systems of our world arise because of human sin—seeking our own interests rather than allowing our hearts and minds to be subservient to God's will. And on this point Christians do have something to say: the prophetic tradition which makes itself heard throughout our canon of Scripture, and in which Jesus himself stands, warns us against these very things.[17] In fact, Jesus stated this as his priority at the very outset of his ministry when, in the synagogue at Nazareth, he read the words of the prophet Isaiah:

> "The Spirit of the Lord is on me,
>
> because he has anointed me
>
> to proclaim good news to the poor.
>
> He has sent me to proclaim freedom for the prisoners
>
> and recovery of sight for the blind,
>
> to set the oppressed free,
>
> to proclaim the year of the Lord's favour."
>
> Then he rolled up the scroll, gave it back to the attendant and sat down. The eyes of everyone in the synagogue were fastened on him. He began by saying to them, "Today this scripture is fulfilled in your hearing." (Luke 4:16–21)

Jesus clearly saw it as his task to bring freedom to those who were victims of all sorts of exploitation. Domination of one group over another, the unjust treatment of those who are disadvantaged in society, the oppression of people who have a different view than our own, and denying people freedom are evils which Jesus

---

17 Gushee and Stassen, *Kingdom Ethics*, 409–26.

proclaims have no place in the kingdom which he will inaugurate throughout his ministry. If we as his disciples believe we are called to continue Jesus's work in this world, speaking out against the injustice that is human trafficking must, surely, be our priority too.

What about Us?

If our message is to be credible, we must first undertake some self-examination. It is one thing to preach against exploitation from our pulpits, to speak out about injustice, and to lobby people in power, but are we modeling the kind of living that we are demanding of others? Put simply, it is easy to decry the actions of others and insist that they conform to certain standards, while being oblivious to or ignoring the fact that our own lives may not stand up to scrutiny.

In order to think about this, we might ask ourselves some questions with regard to our own values as followers of Jesus. *First, we might ask ourselves about our priorities as Christian communities.* Do we really want to work for justice and mercy for the most vulnerable in our societies, or are we more concerned with preserving our own way of life? The Old Testament prophets had a lot to say about those who were more concerned with their own comfort than with exposing corruption, injustice, and oppression in society. The prophet Isaiah is very clear that the people of God should not be complacent:

"The multitude of your sacrifices—
what are they to me?" says the Lord.

"I have more than enough of burnt offerings,
> of rams and fat of fattened animals;
I have no pleasure
> in the blood of bulls and lambs and goats.
When you come to appear before me,
> who has asked this of you,
> this trampling of my courts?
Stop bringing meaningless offerings!
> Your incense is detestable to me.
New Moons, Sabbaths and convocations—
> I cannot bear your worthless assemblies.
Your new moon feasts and your appointed festivals
> I hate with all my being.
They have become a burden to me;
> I am weary of bearing them.
When you spread out your hands in prayer,
> I hide my eyes from you;
Even when you offer many prayers,
> I am not listening.

Your hands are full of blood!

Wash and make yourselves clean.
> Take your evil deeds out of my sight;
> Stop doing wrong.
Learn to do right; seek justice.
> Defend the oppressed.
Take up the cause of the fatherless;
> plead the cause of the widow." (Isa 1:11–17)

What about Us?

Isaiah was speaking out against dishonesty and hypocrisy in the religious life of Judah in the eighth century BC. In his view, the fact that the religious gatherings and early calendar of events were smooth functioning and impressive in scale, was worth nothing when there were people in the land who were being exploited and oppressed.

Isaiah's words are just as applicable to the Christian church today. They challenge us to look at our communities and ask uncomfortable questions. Are we preoccupied with running successful programs and impressive worship services while neglecting the mandate to reach out to the poor? It is so easy for us to become too comfortable and concerned only with the pattern of our own community life, and with our reputation and image, and, at the same time, lose sight of the wider world and its needs. Are we more concerned with the way things are done in church, or with preserving our particular traditions and doctrinal emphases, than with participating in Jesus's work of reaching out to the poor and setting the captives free? Jesus himself made it very clear that compassion and mercy should take precedence over observance of the law. When rebuked by a synagogue leader for healing a woman on the Sabbath, he said:

> You hypocrites! Doesn't each of you on the Sabbath untie your ox or donkey from the stall and lead it out to give it water? Then should not this woman, a daughter of Abraham, whom Satan has kept bound for eighteen long years, be set free on the Sabbath day from what bound her?" (Luke 13:15–16).

If there is one thing that Jesus cannot stand it is hypocrisy among the people of God. The need to be seen as "righteous" is the enemy of our calling to work to bring God's justice and mercy into the world (Matt 23:27). Christians cannot be inward looking—real worship must always result in a concern for the poor both in our own communities and in society as a whole.

Second, *are we in any way colluding with the values which are at the root of human trafficking?* This means, I believe, that we must ask ourselves about our attitude to money and possessions. Are we driven by love of money or love of God? Jesus's teaching is unequivocal—you cannot serve both God and wealth (Matt 6:24). For those of us who live in materialistic, consumerist cultures, this issue can be particularly hard to face. We are constantly under pressure to accumulate property; we continually hear the message that to be successful means to be wealthy.

> We must ask ourselves about our attitude to money and possessions.

It can be easy to fall into the trap of materialism and the desire to accumulate wealth and property, while being blind to the powers that drive us.[18] But as Stassen and Gushee note in their book *Kingdom Ethics*, Jesus urges his followers not to focus on the accumulation of wealth and possessions but to invest our treasures in "God's reign of justice and love through practices of economic generosity and justice-making."[19] We need to ask ourselves what is really driving us in our choice of career, and whether money is assuming too much importance in our lives. For believers, living according to Jesus's teaching that we should not be concerned with what we will eat, drink, or wear is just as much a part of faithful living as is prayer, Bible study, and church attendance. Are we able

---

18 Welby, *Dethroning Mammon*.

19 Gushee and Stassen, *Kingdom Ethics*, 411.

to say that any wealth that we may have belongs to God and not to ourselves, and to share it accordingly?

The exploitation of human beings is not solely a matter of economics, however. It is true that greed is the primary motivating factor for those involved in the trafficking of human beings, but there are other aspects of human nature which contribute to its perpetuation, and Christians cannot claim to be exempt. However uncomfortable it might be to admit, our cultural and religious presuppositions and prejudices can undermine our ability to do to others what we would have them do to us.

This brings us to a third question. *What is our attitude toward others, in particular those who are different from ourselves?* It is much easier to exploit someone if we believe that they are inferior to us because of race, religion, social status, or gender. Much commercial sexual exploitation of women, for example, comes about because they are seen merely as objects. Diana Mao, founder of the Nomi Network in India, reports that in India, young girls are married young, considered to be *paraya dhan*, which means "someone else's wealth."[20] Similarly, people in lower social status groups are more at risk of trafficking than people from higher status groups, while many are targeted as potential for trafficking because they are considered to come from an inferior race or religion.[21]

So, we must examine ourselves about these things too. Attitudes towards race, religion, social status, and gender are very much culture-bound, and we can be unaware of how much our Christian communities are influenced by the cultures in which we

---

20 Moore, Morgan, and Yim, *Ending Human Trafficking*, 28.

21 US State Department, "Trafficking in Persons Report."

find ourselves. Throughout our history, the Christian church has wrestled with the difficult questions of when we should adhere to the norms of the prevailing culture and when we should challenge them. Sometimes this has caused great difficulties within the church, as the case of slavery itself illustrates. Scripture attests to this very problem in the early church; on several occasions Paul had to help his communities to think about what it means to be followers of Jesus in a pagan society, or when there were differences of opinion with regard to religious practices and beliefs.

We can learn from Paul in the letter to the Galatians. In Galatia, the church was being assailed with demands from people that they should conform to certain religious practices amid assertions that those who did not conform were to be considered religiously inferior. You must circumcise the men and observe Jewish law, certain people were insisting, otherwise you can't be considered real believers. The church had already made some changes in response to these demands. Paul, however, was horrified at what was going on and argued strongly against capitulation. He insisted that it was an attempt to place the Galatians under a "yoke of slavery" (Gal 5:1). He objected to the idea that believers from pagan, rather than Jewish, backgrounds were inferior Christians. Moreover, he widened the parameters of his argument and made the extraordinary statement that in baptism *all* become equal:

> There is neither Jew nor Gentile, neither slave nor free, nor is there male and female, for you are all one in Christ Jesus. (Gal 3:28)

These famous words do not mean that Paul considered that racial, religious, social, and gender differences be disregarded altogether. Rather, he wanted the believers in Galatia to realize that among followers of Jesus, the cultural differences which have divided people in the past should no longer do so. He was saying that the cultural and religious presuppositions which can govern our thinking, and whose influence we may not necessarily be aware of, can come to dominate our communities to the extent that our ability to love one another can become compromised. No one group of people is superior or inferior to another for we are "all one in Christ Jesus." A major task for Christian communities is to learn how to live with one another while respecting our differences, how to discern what is important and what is not. As Paul says, certain practices and principles which can seem so precious to us are ultimately unimportant: "The only thing that counts is faith expressing itself through love" (Gal 5:6).

> Among followers of Jesus, the cultural differences which have divided people in the past should no longer do so.

The simple message is this—the church cannot denounce others for being greedy, power driven, and prejudiced if our own communities are scarred by racism, consider that women and girls should be subordinate, and view those who do not share our practices and doctrinal emphases as inferior to ourselves.

A Challenge to Ourselves

It is a privilege to be part of Thierry's life, and to see new life and hope restored to him. But important as practical and emotional support for him and those like him may be, our responsibilities do not stop there. We have seen that as followers of Jesus we are called to "proclaim release to the captives, and recovery of sight to the blind, to set free those who are oppressed" (Luke 4:18 NASB). Besides the practical work of actively getting involved with existing charities which help people like Thierry—supporting their work through prayer and financial giving, and making sure our shopping is responsibly sourced—we also have an obligation to tackle the causes of human trafficking by being a prophetic voice against the values and norms which allow it to flourish.[22]

However, if our voice is to be effective, we must first be willing to examine our own values and ask how far our own communities live up to the standards that Christ requires of his followers. The prophetic tradition demands that our communities be characterized by compassion and mercy rather than complacent,

---

22 Pratt, *Slavery-Free Communities*.

self-serving insularity. Jesus himself challenges us to follow him rather than dedicate ourselves to the accumulation of wealth and possessions, and to be constantly vigilant against any form of hypocrisy and double standards in our own lives and in our communities. Paul's words to the Galatians urge us to reflect on our own attitudes with regard to race, gender, and religious and social difference in our churches. In all these areas we are called to embody and exemplify the values of God's kingdom—the very values which, when absent, contribute to and perpetuate the exploitation and trafficking of human beings.

All these voices in Scripture urge us to ask ourselves how far we prioritize our cultural and religious norms at the expense of the freedom to love and serve each other as Christ himself commanded. Like the Quakers of antebellum America, we can be spurred on by his words: "Do to others do to others what you would have them do to you" (Matt 7:12). These words not only provide the impetus to become actively involved but also to consider if our own Christian communities are living by the values and principles which Scripture teaches should be central to the lives of Jesus's disciples.

> It is vital that we Christians willingly, prayerfully, and humbly examine our attitudes.

These can be difficult questions for churches to acknowledge, let alone address, but we ignore them at our peril, for if our communities do not model what we want to advocate for the rest of the world, our prophetic voice in wider society can only be weakened. It is vital that we Christians willingly, prayerfully, and humbly examine our attitudes regarding money and possessions, social status, and differences of gender, ethnicity, and religion (including our own theological differences) if we are to be credible witnesses for social justice in our world. At the very least, we must be willing to acknowledge our own weaknesses and prejudices as we try to understand where our cultures, both religious and secular, have compromised our ability to love our neighbors, even within our own communities. It takes courage, as the Quakers well knew, to challenge accepted norms, even, and perhaps especially, within the church itself—but if we are to have a prophetic voice in this world and help prevent the enslavement and exploitation of people like Thierry, we must first examine ourselves.

Bibliography

Bales, Kevin. *Ending Slavery: How We Free Today's Slaves*. Berkeley: University of California, 2007.

Carey, Brycchan, and Geoffrey Plank eds. *Quakers and Abolition*. Champaign: University of Illinois Press, 2018.

Carson, Marion L. S. *Human Trafficking, the Bible and the Church: An Interdisciplinary Study*. Eugene, OR: Cascade, 2016.

Christian Organizations Against Trafficking Network. Homepage. https://www.coatnet.org/.

Enrile, Annalisa V. *Ending Human Trafficking and Modern-Day Slavery: Freedom's Journey*. Thousand Oaks: Sage Publications, 2018.

Fairtrade Foundation. "How Can We Tackle Modern Slavery." https://www.fairtrade.org.uk/media-centre/blog/how-can-we-tackle-modern-slavery.

Glasgow City Mission. Homepage. https://www.glasgowcitymission.com/.

Gushee, David P., and Glen H. Stassen. *Kingdom Ethics: Following Jesus in Contemporary Context*. 2nd ed. Grand Rapids, MI: Eerdmans, 2006.

Hemmings, S., S. Jakobowitz, M. Abas, et al. "Responding to the Health Needs of Survivors of Human Trafficking: A Systematic Review." *BMC Health Services Research* 16, no 1 (2016).

International Justice Mission. Homepage. https:www.ijm.org.

Irons, Charles F. *The Origins of Proslavery Christianity: White and Black Evangelicals in Colonial and Antebellum Virginia*. Chapel Hill: University of North Carolina Press, 2008.

Kara, Shiddharth. *Modern Slavery: A Global Perspective*. New York: Columbia University Press, 2017.

Mitchell, Sue. "Ukraine: Thousands of Vulnerable Children Unaccounted For." *BBC*, https://www.bbc.com/news/world-europe-60692442.

Moore, Shayne, Sandra Morgan, and Kimberley McOwen Yim. *Ending Human Trafficking: A Handbook of Strategies for the Church Today*. Downers Grove: IVP Academic, 2022.

Morgan, Kenneth. *Slavery in America: A Reader and Guide*. Edinburgh: Edinburgh University Press, 2005.

Palermo Protocol. https:// ohchr.org/en/instruments-mechanisms/instruments/protocol-prevent-suppress-and-punish-trafficking-persons.

Pratt, Dan, ed. *Slavery-Free Communities: Emerging Theologies and Faith Responses to Modern Slavery*. London: SCM, 2021.

Restore Glasgow Home Page. https://restoreglasgow.org.uk/

Soderlund, Jean R. *Quakers and Slavery: A Divided Spirit*. Princeton: Princeton University Press, 2016.

Tise, Larry A. *Proslavery: A History of the Defense of Slavery in America 1701–1840*. Athens: University of Georgia Press, 1987.

United Nations Human Rights. "Protocol to Prevent, Suppress and Punish Trafficking in Persons Especially Women and Children, supplementing the United Nations Convention against Transnational Organized Crime," Article I.3.a. https://www.ohchr.org/en/instruments-mechanisms/instruments/protocol-prevent-suppress-and-punish-trafficking-persons.

United Nations Office on Drugs and Crime. "Conflict in Ukraine: Key Evidence on Risks of Trafficking in Persons and Smuggling of Migrants." https://www.unodc.org/documents/data-and-analysis/tip/Conflict_Ukraine_TIP_2022.pdf.

United States Department of Labor. "Sweat & Toil: Child Labor, Forced Labor, and Human Trafficking Around the World." www.dol.gov/general/apps/ilab.

United States Department of State Office to Combat Trafficking in Persons. "2022 Trafficking in Persons Report." https://www.state.gov/reports/2022-trafficking-in-persons-report/.

Welby, J. *Dethroning Mammon: Making Money Serve Grace*. London: Bloomsbury Continuum, 2016.

Get Involved

Every book in the Snapshot Series is created to give you an overview of a subject that really matters and to provide links to resources, gatherings, and organizations that will help you move beyond caring to action.

Learn: To help you think further about how Christians might respond to human trafficking see further:

Books

Marion L. S. Carson. *Setting the Captives Free: The Bible and Human Trafficking.* Eugene, OR: Cascade, 2015.

Marion L. S. Carson. *Human Trafficking the Bible and the Church.* Eugene, OR: Cascade, 2016.

Ruth H. Robb and Marion L. S. Carson. *Walk into Freedom: Christian Outreach to People Involved in Commercial Sexual Exploitation.* Burlington: People's Seminary Press, 2021.

Websites

COATNET—https:www.coatnet.org.

Ethical Consumer—https:www.ethicalconsumer.org.

International Christian Alliance on Prostitution—https:www.icapglobal.org.

International Justice Mission—https:www.ijm.org.

Stop the Traffick—https: www. StoptheTraffik.org.

Films

Sound of Freedom. Directed by Alejandro Gomez Monteverde, 2023.

The Whistleblower. Directed by Larysa Kondracki, 2010.

Connect:

Reflection questions for you and/or a group:

1. From a Christian perspective, what is wrong with slavery?

2. How far does the "Golden Rule" help you to understand how you should relate to others?

3. How do you think you and your community can respond to modern slavery? What are the obstacles and barriers to involvement in anti-slavery work?

4. How do you think Paul's words in Galatians 3:28 apply in your community?

5. Examine your own attitudes to differences of race, religion, gender, and class. Are our Christian communities standing up against the norms and values of culture and society?

6. Read Jesus's teachings on money in Matthew 6. How do these words apply in your life?

7. How should we understand these biblical verses (e.g., Lev 25:44–46; 1 Tim 6:1) which seem to support slavery?

Get Involved

Do:

1. Find out as much as you can about modern slavery.

2. Keep up to date: read the most recent "Trafficking in Persons Report."

3. Find out the types of modern slavery which exist in your country and neighborhood.

4. Think about ways in which you can best work against human trafficking, both as an individual and in community. Books such as *Ending Human Trafficking: A Handbook of Strategies for the Church Today* are helpful.

5. Pray for those non-governmental organizations which are active in anti-human trafficking work.

6. Pray for those who are involved in policy and law-making in the field of anti-human trafficking.

visit us at missionbooks.org

Facing Fear
Anna Hampton, Author

Facing Fear is a practical guide for believers who long to have bold, mature courage. Cultivating this courage is necessary to endure wisely for Christ's sake. Anna Hampton integrates exegesis and psychology to explain how humans respond to fear and how the Holy Spirit enables us to make a different choice than our normal. Learning to face our fears, name them, and manage them requires learning specific steps to reduce their impact on us. | Paperback and ePub

Recovering from Traumatic Stress
Stephanie Laite-Lanham and Joyce Pelletier, Authors

Experiencing symptoms of traumatic stress can be debilitating. Post-Traumatic Stress is a normal reaction to an abnormal event. This book teaches about how to recognize the symptoms experienced after a traumatic incident. It offers ways to talk to children and others about traumatic experiences. With God's help, readers who have experienced traumatic situations can begin to regain a sense of peace for themselves and their families. | Paperback and ePub

Abuse of Women in India
Jane McNally, Berkeley Mickelsen, and Alvera Mickelsen, Authors

Jane McNally, who spent most of her life in India, uncovers the problem of abuse in Indian Christian homes with accuracy and authority as well as with pain and passion. The outlined Bible studies help the reader to understand the true biblical and God-given relationship of woman and man, which is the only hope for the redemption of family life, in India and the world. | Paperback

www.ingramcontent.com/pod-product-compliance
Lightning Source LLC
Chambersburg PA
CBHW052207070526
44585CB00017B/2104